# PEACE IN ANXIOUS TIMES

### CALMING ANXIETY THROUGH SCRIPTURE AND PRAYER

Gwen Ebner & Stacey Reeder

Peace in Anxious Times: Calming Anxiety Using Scripture and Prayer
© 2020 by Body and Soul Publishing

All rights reserved. No part of this book may be reproduced, stored in a retrieval system, or transmitted by any means – electronic, mechanical, photocopy, recording, or otherwise – except for brief quotations, without prior permission in writing from the author.

Printed in the United States of America
ISBN: 978-1-946118-16-5

Unless otherwise indicated, Scripture quotations are taken from the Holy Bible, New International Version copyright © 1973, 1978, 1984, 2011 by Biblica, Inc. Used by permission of Zondervan Publishing. All rights reserved worldwide.

Scripture quotations marked NLT are taken from the New Living Translation, copyright © 1996, 2004. Used by permission of Tyndale House. All rights reserved.

Scripture quotations marked ESV are taken from the Holy Bible, English Standard Version, copyright © 2001 by Crossway Bibles. Used by permission. All rights reserved.

Scriptural quotations marked MSG are taken from THE MESSAGE, copyright © 2003 by Eugene Peterson. Used by permission of NavPress Publishing Group. All rights reserved.

Scripture quotations marked TLB are taken from The Living Bible, copyright © 1971 by Tyndale House Foundation. Used by permission of Tyndale House Publishers, Inc., Carol Stream, Illinois 60188. All rights reserved.

# CONTENTS

| | |
|---|---|
| Introduction | 1 |
| Chapter 1<br>Understanding Anxiety | 3 |
| Chapter 2<br>Using Lectio Divina to Calm Anxiety | 11 |
| Chapter 3<br>21 Days of Practicing Lectio Divina | 21 |
| Chapter 4<br>More Scriptures for Practicing Lectio Divina | 65 |
| Chapter 5<br>Other Ways to Manage Anxiety | 71 |
| References | 91 |
| Other Resources | 93 |

# INTRODUCTION

I, Gwen Ebner, was introduced to a life-changing spiritual discipline, Lectio Divina, in 2001 and it transformed the way I studied Scripture. Previous to that time, I had approached Scripture logically because it was what my information-saturated culture had taught me and besides, it was safer.

But Lectio Divina invited me to begin reading the scripture using my mind, then move on to my heart, as I offered my whole self to the process of reading and applying God's Word to my everyday life. Now, the scripture reading had become a two-way conversation with God as he revealed himself to me in surprising ways and as I applied his words to my life.

After writing my first book, Intimate Moments with the Father: Connecting with God in Mind and Heart, God began leading me to make this into a series by using other topics. Little did I know that in the next three years I would personally experience God growing me in the area of anxiety as I struggled through trials like Leaky Gut, digestive issues, Sciatica pain, and caring for an aging parent. What a learning experience this was for me. It was amazing that God was personally preparing me to write this book on replacing anxiety with peace!

I love how patient God is and how he grows us one day at a time as we listen to his voice and follow his leading. Through the formational process and the ideas offered in this book, I invite you to walk on your own journey toward God's peace!

# CHAPTER 1

# Understanding Anxiety

*Written By Stacey Reeder*

Fear. Anxiety. Worry. Panic. We have all experienced these emotions at one time or another. And it is likely since you have chosen to read this book, you may be experiencing the effect of anxiety on your life right now.

Anxiety is a common problem in our day and age. In fact, a study in 2005 by the National Institute of Mental Health found that anxiety was one of the most common mental health issues with 18% of the US population suffering with an anxiety disorder. And, with the seemingly never-ending news reports of all of the global crises happening, there's no wonder why anxiety is running rampant.

The problem with anxiety is that chains accompany it. It tends to hold us captive, paralyze us, and inhibit us from moving forward. It keeps us focused on ourselves and prevents us from being used to our full capacity and purpose. In other words, we become slaves to it.

And this is a trap we can become enslaved to as Christ followers. In fact, Jesus' disciples experienced anxiety and fear even while in the presence of Jesus himself! In the gospel of Mark, an incident is recorded when Jesus and his disciples were in a boat when a great windstorm developed and the waves were breaking into the boat. The disciples frantically awoke Jesus, who had fallen asleep in the back of the boat, and came to their rescue, miraculously calming the wind and the waves. Jesus then asked them, "Why are you so afraid? Have you still no faith?" (Mark 4:40) This demonstrates that fear and anxiety have no limits and can afflict any and all of us.

I, Stacey, have an understanding of the impact of anxiety, not only through my many years in a counseling practice, but also through personal experience. However, I also have experienced freedom from its chains as well.

I don't believe that our anxiety is a surprise to God. Throughout God's Word, you will commonly read phrases such as, "do not worry," "fear not," and "be anxious for nothing." God knew that we would need to hear these commands over and over again. However, just reading and hearing these phrases are sometimes not enough to free us from anxiety. Therefore, I want to give you further clarification about anxiety in order to develop a deeper understanding of the complexity of this emotion.

First, of all, I believe that God gave us the ability to sense fear. Without fear, we could be careless and not exercise caution in dangerous situations. It is fear that keeps us from touching a blazing log in a campfire and scorching our skin; it is fear that keeps a non-swimmer from jumping into deep water and drowning; it is fear that keeps us from approaching a wild animal capable of deadly attack. So fear can be helpful in life.

In that sense, anxiety is like an alarm system. Just as a smoke detector signals the danger of fire, fear and anxiety signal the threat of danger to our body, mind, and emotions. It tells us when danger is near so that we can stay safe. However, this becomes problematic when our fear becomes a False Alarm in rather harmless situations. For instance, we may feel anxious when we have to speak up in a meeting at work or when we have an unexpected home repair or when we have to fly in an airplane after hearing about a plane crash in another part of the world. When that happens, our bodies prepare us for Fight-or- Flight, which typically leaves us shaking, breathing erratically, filled with overwhelming emotion, and completely irrational.

Let me give you a personal example of how a False Alarm fear system can develop. When I was in grade school, I developed a debilitating fear of people vomiting. I realize this is somewhat understandable, as vomit is pretty disgusting. However, this was beyond normal. It first started when a classmate threw up in the library during our class library time. I can remember standing in line waiting to be dismissed, literally shaking uncontrollably. Then followed a series of events that confirmed that vomit was a danger to be avoided: a boy vomited on a twirly carnival ride in MY compartment while it was moving; a girl threw up in a packed car, and we had to ride for what seemed like an eternity with our heads out of the window; a girlfriend threw up in my bed during a sleepover; and a boy threw up as we were exiting the church bus after camp.

These experiences created and confirmed a False Alarm system within me, which caused me to become fiercely avoidant of going to school, riding on amusement park rides, having or going to sleepovers, and being around people in general due to the potential danger that was detected in each of those situations. This became debilitating and frustrating for my family, as well.

Not all False Alarm systems will develop the same way; we all have different experiences and factors that lead to creating a False Alarm. Many times there is a genetic predisposition or a pattern of anxiety regularly modeled before us that can make us more vulnerable. In addition, there may be events, thoughts, attitudes, and perceptions that also contribute to this response.

Ultimately, what I have learned about anxiety is that there is a common thread of loss of control, which becomes the danger our alarm detects. Our worries and concerns are typically about the unknown or the what-ifs or the circumstances outside of our control. And so, in many instances, our anxiety serves as a way to control what is not actually controllable at all.

However, the problem with this is that the more we give attention to our anxiety, worry, and fear, the bigger they grow and the more they consume our thought life. Dr. Caroline Leaf, a neurological psychologist, has devoted a lot of time and energy researching the impact of our thoughts. She has discovered that our thoughts literally take up space in our brains and the more we think negatively, the more space they take up. This is significant considering that our thoughts affect our feelings and behavior.

Let me explain by using the diagram below.

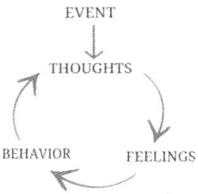

When we experience an event during our day, we instantly and automatically have thoughts and perceptions about the event that allow us to process what just happened. These thoughts then lead to feelings, which then impacts how we behave. As you can see in the diagram above, our thoughts play a crucial role in the False Alarms I referred to earlier; thus, in order to avoid False Alarms and the anxiety that follows, we must have effective thought management.

It will also be helpful if you consider a multi-dimensional approach when working to quiet the anxiety in your life. When anxiety regularly arises as a False Alarm in the absence of a real threat, it can have an adverse effect on your mood, your physical health, your emotional and spiritual wellbeing, as well as your relationship with others. That is why we encourage a holistic approach in this book for dealing with anxiety.

Ironically, if we are going to turn off the False Alarm and be less controlled by our anxiety, we must SURRENDER our need to control. This is where our faith and belief in a God who can do anything is essential. When we cannot trust our circumstances, we can trust a God who loves us immensely and has a plan for our life. When we fear what the future may hold, we can release control to the One who already knows the future. But this is not just a one-time deal.

It is a continuous, moment-by-moment surrender to our Creator, Savior, Redeemer, and Abba Father and an intimate relationship with him.

This is where the spiritual practice of Lectio Divina can be helpful. When we can truly focus our attention on God, who he is, and what he says in his Word, we can begin to find freedom from the grip of anxiety. When his Word speaks to our heart and we prayerfully apply it to our circumstances, the False Alarms of anxiety can be quieted, enabling us to move confidently into our future knowing that he is right beside us.

If you are not familiar with the practice of Lectio Divina, Chapter Two will describe what it is, how to engage in it, and how to apply to your life what the Holy Spirit is saying. And then in Chapter Three you get the opportunity to experience Lectio Divina for thirty days using the topics of anxiety and peace.

In addition, you will find ideas for dealing with anxiety in Chapters Four and Five. These ideas will be approached in a holistic way, looking at the person as a whole being with a Spirit, Soul, and Body.

# CHAPTER 2

# Using LECTIO DIVINA to Calm Anxiety

*Written By Gwen Ebner*

Calming anxiety in your life can be challenging. We have become vulnerable to it for various reasons. Possibly someone has modeled this for you, which was the case for me through my family of origin. Or maybe it has become a lifestyle routine because of the busyness, chaos, and hurts that have taken place in your life.

In the book Stressaholic, Hanna states, "There's no denying it: We are all stressed…Most of us are inundated with more information in one day than someone would have been exposed to throughout their lifetime just a few centuries ago." [1] It is obvious that we all are vulnerable to anxiety!

Sociologists are saying we have so much stimulation today that we have become a culture of distraction. We tend to be distracted, not only by the urgent but also by the trivial. We tend to do a trivial activity rather than spending meaningful moments with others. It has become almost normal to feel overwhelmed and anxious in our highly stimulated, busy lives. In my own experience, it took a relationship crisis and a serious health issue before I became motivated to move from distraction to simplicity and peacefulness.

This process of change will not be something we can merely do by our own effort. We will need to include God in this process so that his power can transform us. The best way to do this is to spend time in his presence. Often we experience anxiety because we are feeling out of control. And control indicates a lack of faith that God can do it; so we grasp to be in control ourselves. However, as we yield our control to him, he will move our anxiety to a sense of peace.

In order to recharge your phone, you must plug it into the power source. In the same way, if we are going to deal with the issue of stress and anxiety, we will need to not only plug into God's power and peace but to unplug from the stimuli of culture.

The 21 Day Lectio Divina experience in Chapter Three can help assist you in not only spending time with God but in meditating and applying his Word to your life. It will involve four steps that include Scripture reading, meditation, application, and prayer. The book of Hebrews tells us that God's Word is alive and full of power (4:12). Through scripture, we are able to hear the voice of God speaking to our hearts and then apply it to our lives. This can have an amazing impact on changing the response we make when anxiety grips us.

Instead of reading a passage of Scripture hurriedly, as we would the daily newspaper or the latest magazine or novel, in Lectio Divina we are invited to read it slowly, meditatively, and a number of times, which helps to draw out its meaning. Through the four steps of Lectio Divina, we have the opportunity to allow God "to be made known to us, speak to us, and shape our lives." [2]

Dom Marmion, a French Benedictine monk, describes the steps of Lectio Divina this way, "We read (Lectio) under the eye of God (meditatio) until the heart is touched (oratio) and leaps to flame (contemplatio)." [3] The first step (Lectio) is where we read the scripture, which most of us see as an exterior exercise. That's why the second step of Lectio Divina moves us to the practice of meditation, which takes place in our inner intellect (our heart). The third step touches us at the level of desire, offering us an opportunity to respond to God's words.

Since Lectio Divina is a free form, method-less method, it will take its own form each time you experience it. Do not try to confine God to a set method; allow him to freely work in you as he chooses. Some days you may spend more time on one part of Lectio Divina than the others. Allow the Spirit to direct you in this. There are a number of ways to practice Lectio Divina but this is the basic form that I have used myself:

You begin with a time of silence in order to "quiet your heart." There are a number of ways to help quiet your heart. For instance, a few cleansing breaths, a body relaxation exercise, picturing yourself in a safe place with God, or listening to peaceful, calming music. After that, you can pray a short prayer acknowledging God's presence and your desire for his guidance. Then you can continue with the four steps below:

Step One (Lectio): Read a brief portion of Scripture slowly several times, listening for a key word or phrase. If you are doing Lectio Divina alone, read the Scripture out loud. Michael Casey calls this "active reading." [4]

Step Two (Meditatio): Meditate, reflecting on the Scripture, especially the word or phrase that stood out the most in the first step. As you attend to the deeper meanings of the text, pay attention to the emotions that surface in you.

This step provides a time of listening and reflecting in order to allow the words to sink from your mind to your heart. Casey reminds us to slow down and savor what we read in order to allow the text to trigger memories and associations that reside below the threshold of our awareness. [5]

Step Three (Oratio): Even though Lectio Divina is a freestyle prayer form from beginning to end, in this step you deliberately ask God for illumination. It may be helpful to ask God why the word and emotions have been evoked in you and how he wants you to apply it to your life.

Tom Gardner suggests we ask some additional questions in this third step: Why do these emotions stir me?" And "Is there anything, Lord, you want to heal in me?" [6]

Step Four (Contemplatio): A period of silence is kept in order to rest in God and in what he has said to you. This step not only allows you to rest in him but also provides a time for committing to become what God wants you to be and do. It will be a continuous process even after you end this formal time of Lectio Divina.

You may notice that the method of Lectio Divina includes moments of reading, reflecting, responding to, and resting in the Word of God with the aim of nourishing and deepening your relationship with God. [7]

Word of Warning: Since Lectio Divina is a spiritual discipline that can draw you closer to God and allow you to prayerfully dialogue with him, don't be surprised when you find yourself distracted. The enemy loves to sidetrack us from spending meaningful time with God.

I have spent over 12 years practicing Lectio Divina once a week with two wonderful friends of mine. I have found it to be a powerful practice when done in a group. So, I offer you this brief outline that Tony Jones suggests for Group Lectio Divina: [8]

Lectio: After a quieting of heart, you can open with prayer acknowledging the presence of God. Then read the passage two or three times, slowly and deliberately. The group is asked to consider a word or phrase that speaks to them. They can then share this with the group.

Meditatio: The scripture is read again two times, possibly in a different translation or maybe even several translations. This time, they are to attend to the emotions or feelings that arise in them. They are then offered a time to share with the group what they have just experienced.

Oratio: The scripture is read again with a longer period of silence. Then, they are encouraged to ask God why this word or feeling has been prompted in them and how they are to apply it to their life. Another time of sharing takes place with people sharing what God is saying to them through the text.

Contemplatio: You can end the session in one of three ways: having each person pray silently, asking one person to pray out loud, or letting people pray for each other.

PREPARING FOR LECTIO

When we begin to practice Lectio Divina, it will be important for us to set aside a time in our day to spend with God. But it is important to realize how central our whole day is in preparing us for this time of Lectio Divina. "If we are constantly being swept off our feet with frantic activity, we will be unable to be attentive at the moment of inward silence." [9]

It will be important for us to establish a "sense of balance in life, an ability to be at peace through the activities of the day, an ability to rest and take the time to enjoy beauty, (and) an ability to pace ourselves." [10] This can happen as we purposefully make an effort to connect with God regularly throughout the day, as we walk, talk, and drive slower, purposing to live with a prayerful heart.

Even though it is not necessary, it may be helpful to use different translations so that you are challenged in the way you look at the scripture. You may want to begin the first step of Lectio Divina with a word-for-word translation, like New King James, English Standard Version, or Amplified.

Then in your second step, you could use a translation that is a balance between word-for-word and thought-for-thought, like New International Version, Holman, New Living Translation, or New Revised Standard Version. Your third step could add the use of a thought-for thought version like the Message or Contemporary English version. When a translation uses word-for-word, it gives you more of an opportunity to understand it for yourself. In comparison, thought-for-thought versions tend to do the interpreting for you. Even though it is more readable, it will have a tendency to close down the process of listening with your own heart for the meaning. [11]

Saint Benedict described Lectio Divina as "cultivating the ability to listen deeply (and) to hear 'with the ear of our heart.'" [12] In order to do this it will be helpful to find a quiet place to read that is free from distractions. It may also be helpful to do it in the same place each day so that it can become your meeting place with God. It will also be important to turn off your cell phone, computer, and other media that may distract you from hearing God's voice.

More important than what Lectio Divina is and how we do it, is that we take time "to do it". Practicing it as an experience for twenty one days can allow it to become a habit in your life. Then you will have the opportunity to choose whether to continue using it as a way of life.

# CHAPTER 3

# 21 Days of Practicing LECTIO DIVINA

This chapter offers you a format for practicing Lectio Divina for the next twenty one days. Each day consists of:

- A suggested scripture for the day
- Some background understanding about the scripture
- The four steps of Lectio Divina with a blank space after each step so that you can more purposefully interact with the scripture [Once you have recorded your responses in writing, a journal record will be available of what God has said to you that day. In the future, you can go back and read what you heard God saying during that time.]
- Finally, there is a quote from a well-known author that picks up one of the themes of the scripture verse as a way to conclude the day's formation time.

## DAY ONE

**Scripture:** Matthew 6:25-34

**Background:** We often worry about the outward necessities we think we need. But Jesus challenges us to seek him, instead of material things, and all our needs will be provided. [Take a few moments to scan through the whole chapter in order to be aware of the context and setting of the text before you begin.]

**The Four Steps of *Lectio Divina*:**

1. ***Lectio*** (read): [Spend a few moments quieting your heart; then prayerfully acknowledge God's presence.] Read the passage out loud 2-3 times slowly. *What is the word or phrase that stands out to you in this passage?*

   _____
   _____
   _____

2. ***Meditatio*** (meditate): Reread the passage slowly in the same or different version. [As you attend to the deeper meaning of the text, pay attention to the feelings and emotions that arise in you. Allow your imagination & senses to be involved as well.] *What did you experience and observe?*

   _____
   _____
   _____

3. ***Oratio*** (prayer): Reread the passage one more time. Actively listen and converse with God about the meaning and application of the scripture. [Ask God why this particular word/phrase and emotions is being evoked in you.] *What did you sense God saying and how does he want to respond?*

_____
_____
_____

4. ***Contemplatio*** (contemplation): A period of silence is kept in order to rest in God. [End with a prayer of commitment to what you have heard God say. Feel free to speak your prayer or to write it out.]

_____
_____
_____

*Worrying does not empty tomorrow of its troubles,*
*It empties today of its strength.*
~ Corrie Ten Boom

*Worrying doesn't take away tomorrow's troubles;*
*it takes away today's peace.*
~ Unknown

## DAY TWO

**Scripture:** Jeremiah 17:5-8

**Background:** Judah has sinned and as a result has drifted away from God. Jeremiah compares the choice and consequence of drifting compared to the choice of relying on him. [Take a few moments to scan through the whole chapter in order to be aware of the context and setting of the text before you begin.]

**The Four Steps of *Lectio Divina*:**
1. ***Lectio*** (read): [Spend a few moments quieting your heart; then prayerfully acknowledge God's presence.] Read the passage out loud 2-3 times slowly. *What is the word or phrase that stands out to you in this passage?*

   _____
   _____
   _____

2. ***Meditatio*** (meditate): Reread the passage slowly in the same or different version. [As you attend to the deeper meaning of the text, pay attention to the feelings and emotions that arise in you. Allow your imagination & senses to be involved as well.] *What did you experience and observe?*

   _____
   _____
   _____

3. ***Oratio*** (prayer): Reread the passage one more time. Actively listen and converse with God about the meaning and application of the scripture. [Ask God why this particular word/phrase and emotions is being evoked in you.] *What did you sense God saying and how does he want to respond?*

_____

_____

_____

4. ***Contemplatio*** (contemplation): A period of silence is kept in order to rest in God. [End with a prayer of commitment to what you have heard God say. Feel free to speak your prayer or to write it out.]

_____

_____

_____

*Trust in the Lord to give you
the power to overcome fear.*
~ Unknown

*Faith and fear are opposite poles.
If a man has the one, he can scarcely
have the other in vigorous operation.
He that has his trust set upon God
does not need to dread anything except the
weakening or the paralyzing of that trust.*
~ Alexander MacLaren

## DAY THREE

**Scripture:** Philippians 4:4-9

**Background:** Is it possible to live in a non-anxious state? In this scripture, Paul reveals some keys to dealing with an anxious heart and how to claim God's peace. [Take a few moments to scan through the whole chapter in order to be aware of the context and setting of the text before you begin.]

**The Four Steps of *Lectio Divina*:**

1. ***Lectio*** (read): [Spend a few moments quieting your heart; then prayerfully acknowledge God's presence.] Read the passage out loud 2-3 times slowly. *What is the word or phrase that stands out to you in this passage?*

   _____
   _____
   _____

2. ***Meditatio*** (meditate): Reread the passage slowly in the same or different version. [As you attend to the deeper meaning of the text, pay attention to the feelings and emotions that arise in you. Allow your imagination & senses to be involved as well.] *What did you experience and observe?*

   _____
   _____
   _____

**3. *Oratio*** (prayer): Reread the passage one more time. Actively listen and converse with God about the meaning and application of the scripture. [Ask God why this particular word/phrase and emotions is being evoked in you.] *What did you sense God saying and how does he want to respond?*

_____
_____
_____

4. Contemplatio (contemplation): A period of silence is kept in order to rest in God. [End with a prayer of commitment to what you have heard God say. Feel free to speak your prayer or to write it out.]

_____
_____
_____

*If the basis of peace is God, the secret of peace is trust.*
*~ J.N. Figgis*

*What a treasure I have in this wonderful peace,*
*buried deep in the heart of my soul.*
*So secure that no power can mine it away,*
*While the years of eternity roll!*
*Peace, peace, wonderful peace,*
*Coming down from the Father above!*
*Sweep over my spirit forever, I pray*
*In fathomless billows of love!*
*~ W. D. Cornell*

## DAY FOUR

**Scripture:** Luke 10:38-42

**Background:** Jesus compares the anxiety of Martha to the peacefulness of Mary. According to Jesus what is the necessary element in dealing with anxiety? [Take a few moments to scan through the whole chapter in order to be aware of the context and setting of the text before you begin.]

**The Four Steps of *Lectio Divina:***
1. *Lectio* (read): [Spend a few moments quieting your heart; then prayerfully acknowledge God's presence.] Read the passage out loud 2-3 times slowly. *What is the word or phrase that stands out to you in this passage?*

    _____
    _____
    _____

2. *Meditatio* (meditate): Reread the passage slowly in the same or different version. [As you attend to the deeper meaning of the text, pay attention to the feelings and emotions that arise in you. Allow your imagination & senses to be involved as well.] What did you experience and observe?

    _____
    _____
    _____

3. ***Oratio*** (prayer): Reread the passage one more time. Actively listen and converse with God about the meaning and application of the scripture. [Ask God why this particular word/phrase and emotions is being evoked in you.] *What did you sense God saying and how does he want to respond?*

_____

_____

_____

4. ***Contemplatio*** (contemplation): A period of silence is kept in order to rest in God. [End with a prayer of commitment to what you have heard God say. Feel free to speak your prayer or to write it out.]

_____

_____

_____

*Pray for the grace to realize that no matter where you are, you are in the presence of the Lord.*
~ Ann Spangler

*Sitting silently at the feet of Jesus is of more worth than all the clatter of Martha's dishes.*
~ Charles Spurgeon

## DAY FIVE

**Scripture:** I Peter 5:6-9

**Background:** Peter quotes from Psalm 55:22 as he offers us advice on dealing with anxiety. [Take a few moments to scan through the whole chapter in order to be aware of the context and setting of the text before you begin.]

**The Four Steps of *Lectio Divina*:**

1. ***Lectio*** (read): [Spend a few moments quieting your heart; then prayerfully acknowledge God's presence.] Read the passage out loud 2-3 times slowly. *What is the word or phrase that stands out to you in this passage?*

   _____

   _____

   _____

2. ***Meditatio*** (meditate): Reread the passage slowly in the same or different version. [As you attend to the deeper meaning of the text, pay attention to the feelings and emotions that arise in you. Allow your imagination & senses to be involved as well.] *What did you experience and observe?*

   _____

   _____

   _____

3. **_Oratio_** (prayer): Reread the passage one more time. Actively listen and converse with God about the meaning and application of the scripture. [Ask God why this particular word/phrase and emotions is being evoked in you.] *What did you sense God saying and how does he want to respond?*

_____

_____

_____

4. **_Contemplatio_** (contemplation): A period of silence is kept in order to rest in God. [End with a prayer of commitment to what you have heard God say. Feel free to speak your prayer or to write it out.]

_____

_____

_____

*Solely wait upon God,*
*placing all your expectations in him.*
~ Charles Spurgeon

*When we put our cares in his hand,*
*he puts his peace in our hearts.*
~ Unknown

*Cast your cares on the Lord and he will sustain you.*
*He will never let the righteous be shaken.*
~ Psalm 55:22 (NIV)

## DAY SIX

**Scripture:** Isaiah 26:1-4

**Background:** Isaiah 26 is a song to God that reveals how we can stay in a place of peace. [Take a few moments to scan through the whole chapter in order to be aware of the context and setting of the text before you begin.]

**The Four Steps of *Lectio Divina:***
1. ***Lectio*** (read): [Spend a few moments quieting your heart; then prayerfully acknowledge God's presence.] Read the passage out loud 2-3 times slowly. *What is the word or phrase that stands out to you in this passage?*

   _____
   _____
   _____

2. ***Meditatio*** (meditate): Reread the passage slowly in the same or different version. [As you attend to the deeper meaning of the text, pay attention to the feelings and emotions that arise in you. Allow your imagination & senses to be involved as well.] *What did you experience and observe?*

   _____
   _____
   _____

3. ***Oratio*** (prayer): Reread the passage one more time. Actively listen and converse with God about the meaning and application of the scripture. [Ask God why this particular word/phrase and emotions is being evoked in you.] *What did you sense God saying and how does he want to respond?*

   _____
   _____
   _____

4. ***Contemplatio*** (contemplation): A period of silence is kept in order to rest in God. [End with a prayer of commitment to what you have heard God say. Feel free to speak your prayer or to write it out.]

   _____
   _____
   _____

*Real contentment must come from within.*
*You and I cannot change*
*or control the world around us,*
*But we can change*
*and control the world within us.*
~ Warren Wiersbe

*God cannot give us a happiness and peace*
*apart from Himself because it is not there.*
*There is no such thing.*
~ C.S. Lewis

## DAY SEVEN

**Scripture:** Isaiah 30:12-15

**Background:** Israel has trusted in oppression and lies, which has resulted in calamity. Instead, God allows them to see the results of a restful heart. [Take a few moments to scan through the whole chapter in order to be aware of the context and setting of the text before you begin.]

**The Four Steps of** *Lectio Divina:*
1. *Lectio* (read): [Spend a few moments quieting your heart; then prayerfully acknowledge God's presence.] Read the passage out loud 2-3 times slowly. *What is the word or phrase that stands out to you in this passage?*

    _____
    _____
    _____

2. *Meditatio* (meditate): Reread the passage slowly in the same or different version. [As you attend to the deeper meaning of the text, pay attention to the feelings and emotions that arise in you. Allow your imagination & senses to be involved as well.] *What did you experience and observe?*

    _____
    _____
    _____

3. ***Oratio*** (prayer): Reread the passage one more time. Actively listen and converse with God about the meaning and application of the scripture. [Ask God why this particular word/phrase and emotions is being evoked in you.] *What did you sense God saying and how does he want to respond?*

_____

_____

_____

4. ***Contemplatio*** (contemplation): A period of silence is kept in order to rest in God. [End with a prayer of commitment to what you have heard God say. Feel free to speak your prayer or to write it out.]

_____

_____

_____

*God has called his creation to find satisfaction*
*in a personal relationship with him,*
*and stop trying to manage the world*
*by conforming it to our expectations,*
*and to allow him to govern his creation.*
*He continues to say through an ancient worship song,*
*"Be still and know that I am God!"*
~ Charles Swindoll

*The quieter you become, the more you can hear.*
~ Rom Dass

## DAY EIGHT

**Scripture:** Isaiah 9:6-7

**Background:** This scripture lists some of the names that describe Jesus, the Messiah. Have you allowed him to fulfill these roles in your life? [Take a few moments to scan through the whole chapter in order to be aware of the context and setting of the text before you begin.]

**The Four Steps of *Lectio Divina*:**
1. *Lectio* (read): [Spend a few moments quieting your heart; then prayerfully acknowledge God's presence.] Read the passage out loud 2-3 times slowly. *What is the word or phrase that stands out to you in this passage?*

   _____
   _____
   _____

2. *Meditatio* (meditate): Reread the passage slowly in the same or different version. [As you attend to the deeper meaning of the text, pay attention to the feelings and emotions that arise in you. Allow your imagination & senses to be involved as well.] *What did you experience and observe?*

   _____
   _____
   _____

3. **Oratio** (prayer): Reread the passage one more time. Actively listen and converse with God about the meaning and application of the scripture. [Ask God why this particular word/phrase and emotions is being evoked in you.] *What did you sense God saying and how does he want to respond?*

_____
_____
_____

4. **Contemplatio** (contemplation): A period of silence is kept in order to rest in God. [End with a prayer of commitment to what you have heard God say. Feel free to speak your prayer or to write it out.]

_____
_____
_____

*There are 256 names given in the Bible for Jesus,*
*And I suppose this was because he was infinitely*
*beyond all that any one name could express.*
~ Billy Sunday


*You don't realize Jesus is all you need*
*until Jesus is all you have.*
~ Tim Keller

## DAY NINE

**Scripture:** Isaiah 35:1-4

**Background:** In this passage Isaiah is encouraging the fearful hearts of the people. After the rebellious nations are destroyed, Jesus will be introduced. [Take a few moments to scan through the whole chapter in order to be aware of the context and setting of the text before you begin.]

### The Four Steps of *Lectio Divina:*

1. *Lectio* (read): [Spend a few moments quieting your heart; then prayerfully acknowledge God's presence.] Read the passage out loud 2-3 times slowly. *What is the word or phrase that stands out to you in this passage?*

   _____
   _____
   _____

2. *Meditatio* (meditate): Reread the passage slowly in the same or different version. [As you attend to the deeper meaning of the text, pay attention to the feelings and emotions that arise in you. Allow your imagination & senses to be involved as well.] *What did you experience and observe?*

   _____
   _____
   _____

**3. *Oratio*** (prayer): Reread the passage one more time. Actively listen and converse with God about the meaning and application of the scripture. [Ask God why this particular word/phrase and emotions is being evoked in you.] *What did you sense God saying and how does he want to respond?*

_____

_____

_____

**4. *Contemplatio*** (contemplation): A period of silence is kept in order to rest in God. [End with a prayer of commitment to what you have heard God say. Feel free to speak your prayer or to write it out.]

_____

_____

_____

*Energize the limp hands,*
*strengthen the rubbery knees.*
*Tell fearful souls, "Courage! Take heart!*
*GOD is here, right here, on his way to put things right*
*And redress all wrongs. He's on his way! He'll save you!*
~ Isaiah 35:4 (MSG)

*If you live in fear of the future because*
*of what happened in your past,*
*you'll end up losing what you have in the present.*
~ Rapidlikes.com

## DAY TEN

**Scripture:** Mark 4:35-41

**Background:** The disciples learn an important lesson in this passage of Mark. They encounter peace in an unexpected situation! [Take a few moments to scan through the whole chapter in order to be aware of the context and setting of the text before you begin.]

**The Four Steps of *Lectio Divina:***

1. ***Lectio*** (read): [Spend a few moments quieting your heart; then prayerfully acknowledge God's presence.] Read the passage out loud 2-3 times slowly. *What is the word or phrase that stands out to you in this passage?*

   _____
   _____
   _____

2. ***Meditatio*** (meditate): Reread the passage slowly in the same or different version. [As you attend to the deeper meaning of the text, pay attention to the feelings and emotions that arise in you. Allow your imagination & senses to be involved as well.] *What did you experience and observe?*

   _____
   _____
   _____

3. ***Oratio*** (prayer): Reread the passage one more time. Actively listen and converse with God about the meaning and application of the scripture. [Ask God why this particular word/phrase and emotions is being evoked in you.] *What did you sense God saying and how does he want to respond?*

_____
_____
_____

4. ***Contemplatio*** (contemplation): A period of silence is kept in order to rest in God. [End with a prayer of commitment to what you have heard God say. Feel free to speak your prayer or to write it out.]

_____
_____
_____

*You are safer with God in the middle of a storm*
*than you are anywhere else without him.*
~ Unknown

*Sometimes he calms the storm*
*with a whispered 'peace be still'.*
*He can settle any sea, but it doesn't mean he will.*
*Sometimes he holds us close*
*and lets the wind and waves go wild.*
*Sometimes he calms the storm and*
*other times he calms his child.*
~ Scott Krippayne

## DAY ELEVEN

**Scripture:** John 14:23-27

**Background:** Jesus death is imminent and to reassure them, he offers them a special gift. It is clear though that they will not be able to obtain this from anyone but him! [Take a few moments to scan through the whole chapter in order to be aware of the context and setting of the text before you begin.]

**The Four Steps of *Lectio Divina*:**
1. ***Lectio*** (read): [Spend a few moments quieting your heart; then prayerfully acknowledge God's presence.] Read the passage out loud 2-3 times slowly. *What is the word or phrase that stands out to you in this passage?*

   _____
   _____
   _____

2. ***Meditatio*** (meditate): Reread the passage slowly in the same or different version. [As you attend to the deeper meaning of the text, pay attention to the feelings and emotions that arise in you. Allow your imagination & senses to be involved as well.] *What did you experience and observe?*

   _____
   _____
   _____

3. ***Oratio*** (prayer): Reread the passage one more time. Actively listen and converse with God about the meaning and application of the scripture. [Ask God why this particular word/phrase and emotions is being evoked in you.] *What did you sense God saying and how does he want to respond?*

_____
_____
_____

4. ***Contemplatio*** (contemplation): A period of silence is kept in order to rest in God. [End with a prayer of commitment to what you have heard God say. Feel free to speak your prayer or to write it out.]

_____
_____
_____

*When Christ died he left a will in which he gave his soul to his Father, his body to Joseph of Arimathea, his clothes to the soldiers, and his mother to John. But to his disciples, who had left all to follow him, he left not silver or gold, but something far better – his PEACE!*
~ Matthew Henry

*If our minds are stayed upon God, his peace will rule the affairs entertained by our minds. If, on the other hand, we allow our minds to dwell on the cares of this world, God's peace will be far from our thoughts.*
~ Woodrow Kroll

## DAY TWELVE

**Scripture:** John 20: 19-23

**Background:** Jesus appears for the first time after the resurrection and the words he offers to the disciples are the same ones he spoke to them just before he died. [Take a few moments to scan through the whole chapter in order to be aware of the context and setting of the text before you begin.]

**The Four Steps of *Lectio Divina:***
1. ***Lectio*** (read): [Spend a few moments quieting your heart; then prayerfully acknowledge God's presence.] Read the passage out loud 2-3 times slowly. *What is the word or phrase that stands out to you in this passage?*

   _____
   _____
   _____

2. ***Meditatio*** (meditate): Reread the passage slowly in the same or different version. [As you attend to the deeper meaning of the text, pay attention to the feelings and emotions that arise in you. Allow your imagination & senses to be involved as well.] *What did you experience and observe?*

   _____
   _____
   _____

3. ***Oratio*** (prayer): Reread the passage one more time. Actively listen and converse with God about the meaning and application of the scripture. [Ask God why this particular word/phrase and emotions is being evoked in you.] *What did you sense God saying and how does he want to respond?*

_____
_____
_____

4. ***Contemplatio*** (contemplation): A period of silence is kept in order to rest in God. [End with a prayer of commitment to what you have heard God say. Feel free to speak your prayer or to write it out.]

_____
_____
_____

*Seek true peace – not in earth but in heaven;*
*not in men, nor in any other creature,*
*but in God alone.*
~ Thomas a Kempis

*The Spirit of God has the habit of taking*
*the words of Jesus out of their scriptural setting*
*and putting them into the setting*
*of our personal lives.*
~ Oswald Chambers

## DAY THIRTEEN

**Scripture:** Galatians 5:22-25

**Background:** Paul gives us a list of the Fruit of the Spirit, peace being one of them. Have you allowed God to grow this fruit in your life? [Take a few moments to scan through the whole chapter in order to be aware of the context and setting of the text before you begin.]

### The Four Steps of *Lectio Divina:*

1. ***Lectio*** (read): [Spend a few moments quieting your heart; then prayerfully acknowledge God's presence.] Read the passage out loud 2-3 times slowly. *What is the word or phrase that stands out to you in this passage?*

   _____
   _____
   _____

2. ***Meditatio*** (meditate): Reread the passage slowly in the same or different version. [As you attend to the deeper meaning of the text, pay attention to the feelings and emotions that arise in you. Allow your imagination & senses to be involved as well.] *What did you experience and observe?*

   _____
   _____
   _____

3. ***Oratio*** (prayer): Reread the passage one more time. Actively listen and converse with God about the meaning and application of the scripture. [Ask God why this particular word/phrase and emotions is being evoked in you.] *What did you sense God saying and how does he want to respond?*

_____
_____
_____

4. ***Contemplatio*** (contemplation): A period of silence is kept in order to rest in God. [End with a prayer of commitment to what you have heard God say. Feel free to speak your prayer or to write it out.]

_____
_____
_____

*Fruit is always the miraculous, the created;*
*it is never the result of willing, but always a growth.*
*The fruit of the Spirit is a gift of God,*
*and only he can produce it.*
*They who bear it know as little about it*
*as the tree knows of its fruit.*
*They know only the power of him*
*on whom their life depends*
~ Dietrich Bonhoeffer

*Let the peace of Christ rule in your hearts.*
~ Colossians 3:15 (NIV)

## DAY FOURTEEN

**Scripture:** Colossians 3:12-15

**Background:** Paul is challenging us to put on seven spiritual garments, including the peace of Christ. How could this make a difference in your life? [Take a few moments to scan through the whole chapter in order to be aware of the context and setting of the text before you begin.]

### The Four Steps of *Lectio Divina:*
1. ***Lectio*** (read): [Spend a few moments quieting your heart; then prayerfully acknowledge God's presence.] Read the passage out loud 2-3 times slowly. *What is the word or phrase that stands out to you in this passage?*

   _____
   _____
   _____

2. ***Meditatio*** (meditate): Reread the passage slowly in the same or different version. [As you attend to the deeper meaning of the text, pay attention to the feelings and emotions that arise in you. Allow your imagination & senses to be involved as well.] *What did you experience and observe?*

   _____
   _____
   _____

3. ***Oratio*** (prayer): Reread the passage one more time. Actively listen and converse with God about the meaning and application of the scripture. [Ask God why this particular word/phrase and emotions is being evoked in you.] *What did you sense God saying and how does he want to respond?*

_____

_____

_____

4. ***Contemplatio*** (contemplation): A period of silence is kept in order to rest in God. [End with a prayer of commitment to what you have heard God say. Feel free to speak your prayer or to write it out.]

_____

_____

_____

*It is confidence in the invariably overriding intention of God for our good that secures us in peace and joy. We must be sure of that intention if we are to be free and able, like Joseph, to simply do what we know to be right.*
~ Willard

*One of the secrets of inner peace is the practice of compassion.*
~ PictureQuotes.com

## DAY FIFTEEN

**Scripture:** John 14:23-27

**Background:** Jesus informs his followers that he is leaving a legacy for them that will make a difference in their lives. [Take a few moments to scan through the whole chapter in order to be aware of the context and setting of the text before you begin.]

### The Four Steps of *Lectio Divina:*

1. ***Lectio*** (read): [Spend a few moments quieting your heart; then prayerfully acknowledge God's presence.] Read the passage out loud 2-3 times slowly. *What is the word or phrase that stands out to you in this passage?*

   _____
   _____
   _____

2. ***Meditatio*** (meditate): Reread the passage slowly in the same or different version. [As you attend to the deeper meaning of the text, pay attention to the feelings and emotions that arise in you. Allow your imagination & senses to be involved as well.] *What did you experience and observe?*

   _____
   _____
   _____

3. ***Oratio*** (prayer): Reread the passage one more time. Actively listen and converse with God about the meaning and application of the scripture. [Ask God why this particular word/phrase and emotions is being evoked in you.] *What did you sense God saying and how does he want to respond?*

_____
_____
_____

4. ***Contemplatio*** (contemplation): A period of silence is kept in order to rest in God. [End with a prayer of commitment to what you have heard God say. Feel free to speak your prayer or to write it out.]

_____
_____
_____

*When you put your cares in God's hands*
*he puts his peace in your heart.*
~ Worshipgift

*Those who leave everything in*
*GOD'S HAND*
*will eventually see*
*God's hand in everything.*
~ Godsgracefulness.com

## DAY SIXTEEN

**Scripture:** Psalm 4:1-8

**Background:** David had plenty of opportunities to experience distress, but in spite of it, he is able to encounter God's peace. [Take a few moments to scan through the whole chapter in order to be aware of the context and setting of the text before you begin.]

### The Four Steps of *Lectio Divina:*
1. *Lectio* (read): [Spend a few moments quieting your heart; then prayerfully acknowledge God's presence.] Read the passage out loud 2-3 times slowly. *What is the word or phrase that stands out to you in this passage?*

   _____
   _____
   _____

2. *Meditatio* (meditate): Reread the passage slowly in the same or different version. [As you attend to the deeper meaning of the text, pay attention to the feelings and emotions that arise in you. Allow your imagination & senses to be involved as well.] *What did you experience and observe?*

   _____
   _____
   _____

3. ***Oratio*** (prayer): Reread the passage one more time. Actively listen and converse with God about the meaning and application of the scripture. [Ask God why this particular word/phrase and emotions is being evoked in you.] *What did you sense God saying and how does he want to respond?*

   _____
   _____
   _____

4. ***Contemplatio*** (contemplation): A period of silence is kept in order to rest in God. [End with a prayer of commitment to what you have heard God say. Feel free to speak your prayer or to write it out.]

   _____
   _____
   _____

*Sleep in peace tonight.*
*God is bigger than anything you*
*will face tomorrow.*
~ Patheos.com

*10 Things God wants you to remember:*
*I will give you rest. I will strengthen you. I will answer you.*
*I believe in you. I will bless you. I am for you.*
*I will not fail you. I will provide for you.*
*I will be with you. I love you.*
~ Unknown

## DAY SEVENTEEN

**Scripture:** Psalm 131:1-3

**Background:** David didn't claim to have all the answers. but he discovered that his attitude of confidence in God had a positive affect on his soul. [Take a few moments to scan through the whole chapter in order to be aware of the context and setting of the text before you begin.]

**The Four Steps of *Lectio Divina:***
1. ***Lectio*** (read): [Spend a few moments quieting your heart; then prayerfully acknowledge God's presence.] Read the passage out loud 2-3 times slowly. *What is the word or phrase that stands out to you in this passage?*

   _____
   _____
   _____

2. ***Meditatio*** (meditate): Reread the passage slowly in the same or different version. [As you attend to the deeper meaning of the text, pay attention to the feelings and emotions that arise in you. Allow your imagination & senses to be involved as well.] *What did you experience and observe?*

   _____
   _____
   _____

3. ***Oratio*** (prayer): Reread the passage one more time. Actively listen and converse with God about the meaning and application of the scripture. [Ask God why this particular word/phrase and emotions is being evoked in you.] *What did you sense God saying and how does he want to respond?*

_____
_____
_____

4. ***Contemplatio*** (contemplation): A period of silence is kept in order to rest in God. [End with a prayer of commitment to what you have heard God say. Feel free to speak your prayer or to write it out.]

_____
_____
_____

*Quiet the mind and the soul will speak.*
~ Ma Jaya Sati Bhagavati

*Oh that you would keep silent,*
*and it would be your wisdom!*
~ Job 13:5 (ESV)

*Worry has been compared to a rocking chair.*
*You can rock as much as you want,*
*But you will never get anywhere!*
~ Unknown

## DAY EIGHTEEN

**Scripture:** Matthew 14:22-33

**Background:** In this passage we see a parallel between the fear of the disciples and the peace of Jesus. Jesus asks Peter an important question and offers the disciples some helpful advice. [Take a few moments to scan through the whole chapter in order to be aware of the context and setting of the text before you begin.]

**The Four Steps of *Lectio Divina*:**
1. ***Lectio*** (read): [Spend a few moments quieting your heart; then prayerfully acknowledge God's presence.] Read the passage out loud 2-3 times slowly. *What is the word or phrase that stands out to you in this passage?*

    _____
    _____
    _____

2. ***Meditatio*** (meditate): Reread the passage slowly in the same or different version. [As you attend to the deeper meaning of the text, pay attention to the feelings and emotions that arise in you. Allow your imagination & senses to be involved as well.] *What did you experience and observe?*

    _____
    _____
    _____

3. ***Oratio*** (prayer): Reread the passage one more time. Actively listen and converse with God about the meaning and application of the scripture. [Ask God why this particular word/phrase and emotions is being evoked in you.] *What did you sense God saying and how does he want to respond?*

_____
_____
_____

4. ***Contemplatio*** (contemplation): A period of silence is kept in order to rest in God. [End with a prayer of commitment to what you have heard God say. Feel free to speak your prayer or to write it out.]

_____
_____
_____

*In the midst of chaos and confusion, the peace of God is the best resource and companion you can have.*
~ Gwen Ebner

*God's peace is supernatural.
It overrides personality and temperament.
It is as sure and certain and effective for one person as for another because it comes from the heart of God rather than from the human heart.*
~ Unknown

## DAY NINETEEN

**Scripture:** Psalm 23:1-4

**Background:** The Psalmist uses the image of a shepherd to bring help and comfort to his people. [Take a few moments to scan through the whole chapter in order to be aware of the context and setting of the text before you begin.]

### The Four Steps of *Lectio Divina:*
1. ***Lectio*** (read): [Spend a few moments quieting your heart; then prayerfully acknowledge God's presence.] Read the passage out loud 2-3 times slowly. *What is the word or phrase that stands out to you in this passage?*

   _____
   _____
   _____

2. ***Meditatio*** (meditate): Reread the passage slowly in the same or different version. [As you attend to the deeper meaning of the text, pay attention to the feelings and emotions that arise in you. Allow your imagination & senses to be involved as well.] *What did you experience and observe?*

   _____
   _____
   _____

3. ***Oratio*** (prayer): Reread the passage one more time. Actively listen and converse with God about the meaning and application of the scripture. [Ask God why this particular word/phrase and emotions is being evoked in you.] *What did you sense God saying and how does he want to respond?*

_____

_____

_____

4. ***Contemplatio*** (contemplation): A period of silence is kept in order to rest in God. [End with a prayer of commitment to what you have heard God say. Feel free to speak your prayer or to write it out.]

_____

_____

_____

*Nature is the best medicine for serenity.*
*Peace, calmness, stillness. It's good for the heart.*
~ Karen Madewell

*Silence has a mysterious calming effect,*
*allowing your soul to be at peace with your thoughts.*
~ Anthony Douglas Williams

## DAY TWENTY

**Scripture:** Psalm 37:3-7

**Background:** David had suffered a great deal at the hands of deceitful men. Now as wise old man, he shares advice on how to react when you encounter these types of situations. [Take a few moments to scan through the whole chapter in order to be aware of the context and setting of the text before you begin.]

**The Four Steps of *Lectio Divina*:**
1. ***Lectio*** (read): [Spend a few moments quieting your heart; then prayerfully acknowledge God's presence.] Read the passage out loud 2-3 times slowly. *What is the word or phrase that stands out to you in this passage?*

    _____
    _____
    _____

2. ***Meditatio*** (meditate): Reread the passage slowly in the same or different version. [As you attend to the deeper meaning of the text, pay attention to the feelings and emotions that arise in you. Allow your imagination & senses to be involved as well.] *What did you experience and observe?*

    _____
    _____
    _____

3. ***Oratio*** (prayer): Reread the passage one more time. Actively listen and converse with God about the meaning and application of the scripture. [Ask God why this particular word/phrase and emotions is being evoked in you.] *What did you sense God saying and how does he want to respond?*

   _____
   _____
   _____

4. ***Contemplatio*** (contemplation): A period of silence is kept in order to rest in God. [End with a prayer of commitment to what you have heard God say. Feel free to speak your prayer or to write it out.]

   _____
   _____
   _____

*To trust means to obey willingly*
*without knowing the end from the beginning.*
*To produce fruit, your trust in the Lord*
*must be more powerful and enduring than your confidence*
*in your own personal feelings or experience.*
~ Richard G. Scott

*If you learn to trust God – really trust him –*
*with your whole being,*
*Then nothing can separate you from his Peace.*
~ Sarah Young

## DAY TWENTY-ONE

**Scripture:** Exodus 14:10-14

**Background:** The Israelites have left Egypt and are heading toward the Red Sea, only to discover that Pharaoh is coming after them. When the Israelites became terrified, Moses offers them valuable advice. [Take a few moments to scan through the whole chapter in order to be aware of the context and setting of the text before you begin.]

### The Four Steps of *Lectio Divina:*

1. *Lectio* (read): [Spend a few moments quieting your heart; then prayerfully acknowledge God's presence.] Read the passage out loud 2-3 times slowly. *What is the word or phrase that stands out to you in this passage?*

   _____
   _____
   _____

2. *Meditatio* (meditate): Reread the passage slowly in the same or different version. [As you attend to the deeper meaning of the text, pay attention to the feelings and emotions that arise in you. Allow your imagination & senses to be involved as well.] *What did you experience and observe?*

   _____
   _____
   _____

3. ***Oratio*** (prayer): Reread the passage one more time. Actively listen and converse with God about the meaning and application of the scripture. [Ask God why this particular word/phrase and emotions is being evoked in you.] *What did you sense God saying and how does he want to respond?*

_____

_____

_____

4. ***Contemplatio*** (contemplation): A period of silence is kept in order to rest in God. [End with a prayer of commitment to what you have heard God say. Feel free to speak your prayer or to write it out.]

_____

_____

_____

> *When GOD pushes you to the edge*
> *of difficulty, trust HIM fully*
> *because two things will happen.*
> *Either he will catch you when you fall*
> *OR he will teach you how to fly.*
> *~ PictureQuotes.com*

> *Trusting God completely means having faith*
> *that he knows what's best for your life.*
> *~ PictureQuotes.com*

# God's Presence

*Anxious thoughts meander about
and crisscross in your brain,
But trusting God brings you
directly into his presence.
(Sarah Young)*

*Listen
Be still, and know
that I am God.
(Psalm 46:10)*

# CHAPTER 4

# More Scriptures For Practicing
# LECTIO DIVINA

In this chapter, you will find extra scriptures for doing Lectio Divina. We have repeated the four steps of Lectio Divina for your use as well. We encourage you to journal your responses. This will provide a record of what God is saying to you each day.

You will never use up your resources in practicing Lectio Divina because God's Word is inexhaustible. It will be useful at times to revisit scriptures you have already read since God's Word is alive and always speaking something fresh to us through his Spirit!

The first page of additional scriptures will pertain to anxiety and peace and are listed on a chart. The next page will have scriptures pertaining to "Your Identity in Christ." It will refresh your understanding of who you are in Christ, which is so important to your relationship with him.

You may also want to use scriptures from the first book of this series, Intimate Moments with the Father: Connecting with God in Mind and Heart. In addition, feel free to choose your own scriptures with topics that you want to study. May God bless you as you continue meeting with him each day through this wonderful practice of Lectio Divina!

## THE FOUR STEPS OF LECTIO DIVINA

The Four Steps of Lectio Divina:

1. Lectio (read): [Spend a few moments quieting your heart; then prayerfully acknowledge God's presence.] Read the passage out loud 2-3 times slowly. What is the word or phrase that stands out to you in this passage?
2. Meditatio (meditate): Reread the passage slowly in the same or different version. [As you attend to the deeper meaning of the text, pay attention to the feelings and emotions that arise in you. Allow your imagination & senses to be involved as well.] What did you experience and observe?
3. Oratio (prayer): Reread the passage one more time. Actively listen and converse with God about the meaning and application of the scripture. [Ask God why this particular word/phrase and emotions is being evoked in you.] What did you sense God saying and how does he want to respond?
4. Contemplatio (contemplation): A period of silence is kept in order to rest in God. [End with a prayer of commitment to what you have heard God say. Feel free to speak your prayer or to write it out.]

## ADDITIONAL SCRIPTURES FOR LECTIO DIVINA

Colossians 3:14-17
Romans 15:12-13
Psalm 56:3
Isaiah 53:4-6
Isaiah 54:10
Mark 6:45-51
Proverbs 12:24-26
Romans 8:14-16
Psalm 27:1-5
Psalm 33:18-19
Isaiah 41:10-13
Isaiah 43:1-5
Mark 5:25-34
Luke 2:8-11
II Thessalonians 3:16
II Timothy 1:6-7
Hebrews 13:5-6
I John 4:17-19
Psalm 50:14-15
Romans 15:13
I Timothy 2:1-5
Psalm 46:10
Isaiah 28:11-13
Psalm 4:7-8
Psalm 29:10-11
Isaiah 53:4-5
Psalm 139:23-24
Ecclesiastes 2:21-23
Isaiah 50:7-10

## ADDITIONAL LECTIO DIVINA
### "Your Identity in Christ"

| | |
|---|---|
| I am loved with an everlasting love | Jer. 31:3 |
| I am fearfully & wonderfully made | Ps. 139:13-14 |
| I am a new creation in Christ | II Cor. 5:17-19 |
| I am redeemed & forgiven by grace | Eph. 1:7-8 |
| I am set free in Christ | Gal. 5:1 |
| I am chosen, holy & blameless | Eph. 1:3-4 |
| I am righteousness of God in Christ | II Cor. 5:21 |
| I have a purpose & plan for my life | Jer. 29:11-13 |
| I am a person of peace | Phil. 4:6-7 |
| I am made complete in Christ | Col. 2:9-10 |
| I am held in the arms of God | Deut. 33:27 |
| I am the apple of God's eye | Deut. 32:9-11 |
| I am a citizen of heaven | Phil. 3:20-21 |
| I am treasured by God | Deut. 7:6 |
| I am the delight of God | Zeph. 3:17 |
| I have access to God through faith | Eph. 3:12 |
| I am a child of God | Jn. 1:12-13 |
| I am a friend of Jesus | Jn. 15:15 |
| I am crucified with Christ | Gal. 6:6-7 |
| I am united with Christ and one in Spirit with him | I Cor. 6:17 |

# CHAPTER 5

# Other Ways To Manage Anxiety

**ANXIETY ASSESSMENT**

Anxiety is a very broad term that can cover a variety of emotions. You may, in fact, not realize that anxiety is a problem for you since it does not present itself in obvious ways. In order to help you identify if anxiety may be present in your life, consider the following checklist of various feelings and physical symptoms that may be linked to anxiety.

*Please consider these symptoms with care; they are not intended to diagnose. See your doctor or mental health professional for further information and diagnosis.

Do you feel:
- ☐ Uneasy
- ☐ Apprehensive
- ☐ Overly cautious
- ☐ Urge to control (circumstances or others)
- ☐ Hesitant
- ☐ Tense

- ☐ Nervous
- ☐ Worried
- ☐ Edgy
- ☐ Distressed
- ☐ Scared
- ☐ Frightened
- ☐ Agitated
- ☐ Afraid
- ☐ Shocked
- ☐ Alarmed
- ☐ Overwhelmed
- ☐ Frantic
- ☐ Panic stricken
- ☐ Terrified
- ☐ Hyper vigilant

Have you Experienced:
- ☐ Chest pains
- ☐ Tightness in chest
- ☐ Heart palpitations
- ☐ Frequent headaches
- ☐ Frequent stomach issues
- ☐ "Butterflies" in stomach
- ☐ Diarrhea
- ☐ Tightness in shoulders or jaw
- ☐ Mind racing
- ☐ Difficulty concentrating
- ☐ Difficulty sleeping

- ☐ Easily fatigued
- ☐ Restlessness
- ☐ Shallow breathing
- ☐ Nervous twitching
- ☐ "Emotional" eating

Reflect on the items you checked in each section above.
- *Which of the above feelings and symptoms occur most often in your life?*
- *What might be a trigger for these? Where and why?*
- *Try journaling when you notice a pattern or trigger*

## OTHER WAYS TO MANAGE ANXIETY

In this chapter, you will find ideas that embrace all parts of yourself – your physical body, spiritual being, and your emotions. That is because anxiety will impact all areas of your body. So looking at this issue in a holistic way is very important.

### Breathing Techniques

Your breath is always accessible and should be the first thing you become aware of when you are anxious. Your body reacts by getting tense, causing you to hold your breath or shallow breathe, producing the symptoms of hyperventilating which makes you more anxious.

Breathing exercises activate your body's relaxation response and help your body go from the Fight-or-Flight response of the sympathetic nervous system to the relaxed response of the parasympathetic system.

It is usually helpful to exhale first when you are doing these techniques so that when you take in air, you make room for it by clearing your lungs.

Here are some breathing techniques to try:

*Deep Breathing* (Imagine your stomach as a balloon)
1. To empty your lungs, exhale through your mouth as long as you can (pulling in your stomach)
2. Take a slow deep breath in through your nose (to the count of 4), beginning in your lower stomach, then your lungs, and finally your chest (notice how your stomach expands as you breathe in)
3. Pause 4 seconds
4. Exhale through your nose (to the count of 4) by pulling your belly in
5. Pause 4 seconds again
6. Repeat steps 2-5 several times

*Foursquare Breathing* (Maggie Phillips)
1. Inhale for a count of four (stomach expands)

2. Hold your breath for a count of four
3. Exhale to the count of four (stomach deflates)
4. Hold your breath for a count of four again
5. Repeat steps 1-4 several times

*Circular Breathing* (Maggie Phillips)
1. Allow your breath to flow UP one side of your body as you inhale in through your nose
2. Then exhale as you go down the other side of your body
3. Repeat for four times; then reverse the order (beginning from the other side of the body

*Stress Relief for relaxing quickly*
1. Place your arms down along the sides of your body
2. As you inhale deeply through your nose, stretch your arms out and up as if to form a V shape
3. Then exhale slowly through your nose and bring your arms back down to your side
4. Repeat this as many times as you feel necessary

*Breathe and Let Go* (Sally Kempton)
1. Observe what part of your body feels tight
2. Close your eyes and imagine breathing into this body part with the thought, "Let go"

**Breath Prayer**
*This combines the calming effect of breath along with words of Scripture.*
1. Get seated comfortably
2. Slowly inhale to the count of 4 and then exhale to the count of 4 to set the pattern of breathing
3. Continue the same breathing pattern, but add a phrase of scripture in rhythm with your breathing
4. Focus during every repetition on the meaning of the words, praying or meditating on them with the heart
5. Try doing a Breath Prayer with Psalm 46:10, a scripture that connects with the topic of anxiety:
    - Inhale to the words, "Be still and know"
    - Exhale to the words, "that I am God"

**Essential Oils and Teas**
- The use of essential oils can have a calming-type effect on your body
- These are some good choices for anxiety from a company called Young Living: Peace and Calming, Stress Relief, Lavender, Citrus Fresh, Ylang Ylang, and Ruta VaLa
- Try using them on yourself, as well as putting lavender sachets in your drawers and closets

- Diffusing essential oils into the air can also be helpful to do when you are having a stressful day
- If you have an anxious person visiting in your home, try diffusing a calming essential oil to help both of you
- Herbal Teas can also be calming. You might want to try: Chamomile, Lemon balm, Lavender, and Valerian Root tea

**Health Tips**
- Avoid sugar and processed carbs because they initially give you a surge of energy but then make your blood sugar drop leaving you lethargic, depressed, and more vulnerable to anxiety
- Avoid junk food because it offers very few of the nutrients needed as a defense against anxiety
- Caffeine can keep you awake at night which results in anxiety
- Green Tea may be helpful in taking off the edge of anxiety because it contains L-theanine, an amino acid that has been shown to help induce quiet and calm
- Healthy foods have Vitamin B, magnesium, calcium, and Omega 3 fatty acids which can be calming

*Supplements to help with anxiety:*
1. Magnesium is an anti-stress mineral and most of us are deficient in it
2. Calcium is a calming mineral for your nervous system
3. B Vitamin deficiency is often linked to anxiety and depression

Note: If you are unsure if you should take these supplements, check with your doctor

## Meditation, Visualization, and Mindfulness

**Meditation** and meditate are words that can be found approximately 20 times in scripture. This is King David's desire concerning the meditation of his heart, "Let the words of my mouth and the meditation of my heart be acceptable in your sight, O Lord" (Ps. 19:14, ESV). The Message says it this way, "These are the words of my mouth and what I chew on and pray" (Ps. 19:14, Message).

Meditating can be described as chewing on God's Word prayerfully, but it might also be described as reflecting, pondering, thinking about, or fixing our mind on God or his Word. Paul reminds us to allow the word of God to make its home in us so it permeates every aspect of our being (Col. 3:16). When the words of scripture become a part of us, they are more accessible when we are anxious or afraid.

You may want to begin your meditation time by taking a calming breath or by listening to a worship song. The Psalmist offers us a promise when we place our focus on the Lord, "I have set the Lord always before me; because he is at my right hand, I shall not be shaken" (Ps. 16:8, ESV). We will not be shaken or defeated when our eyes are on the Lord!

When anxious, try meditating on some of the scriptures in the 21-day Lectio experience in Chapter Three. For instance, try meditating on Philippians 4:6-7 where Paul describes how to get rid of anxiety: Engage your mind and heart by rejoicing, foster a gentle spirit, and embrace the assurance that God is always with you and near. Then present your anxieties to him, releasing them to him. End the time of meditation by being thankful. There is no set pattern when you meditate; the key element is to focus on Jesus.

The songwriter, Helen Lemmel, wrote a song that paints a picture of these elements of meditation: "Turn your eyes upon Jesus, Look full in his wonderful face. And the things of earth will grow strangely dim, In the light of his glory and grace." (Public Domain)

In this song, Lemmel gives us these directives:

1. Focus on Jesus (turn your eyes upon Jesus)
2. Let go of all other thoughts (look full in his face); Hearing his voice will require that you have a quiet heart which can only happen if you avoid distractions and multi-tasking when you are spending time with God
3. You will be so refreshed in his presence that other things will seem less important (the things of earth will grow strangely dim)

**Visualization** is another form of meditation, which uses pictures or images. You may want to image a peaceful place you have experienced, a calming nature scene, or Jesus holding you in his arms or with his arms underneath you (Deut. 33:27).

It may also be helpful to visualize the words of scripture. For example: "Cast all your cares on him, because he cares for you" (I Pet. 5:7, NIV). When Peter used the term cast in this scripture, he was referring to the process of casting a fishing pole out and away from you. Can you visualize yourself doing that with your cares?

**Mindfulness** is a form of meditation as well. The Psalmist introduces us to the word mindful when he says, "What is man that you (God) are mindful of him"

(Ps. 8:4, ESV)? This refers to God remembering and thinking about us. We are on his mind!

But being mindful is also a concept that is important for us. It helps us pay attention to what is happening immediately in front of us in the present, instead of getting stuck in the past or worrying about the future ahead. The scriptures remind us to "forget the past" (Phil. 3:13, NLT) and to avoid "worrying about tomorrow" (Matt. 6:34, NLT) for we can only truly experience God in this moment. He "was" in our past and "will be" in our future, but right now he "is" in this moment. As you practice focusing on the present moment, you will be more aware of your thoughts and feelings and what your senses are observing.

We all have thoughts that flash through our minds, but it is what we do with those thoughts that matter. Awareness can help us recognize when we are anxious and what has caused us to be anxious. The quicker we become aware of our anxiety, the more likely we will avoid being consumed by it and prevent its spiraling effect on us. God "will keep in perfect peace all those who trust in him, whose thoughts turn often to the Lord" (Isa. 26:3, TLB, bolded letters added).

Mindfulness allows us to observe our thoughts or feelings and merely notice them without judging them or judging ourselves. This way we can acknowledge them, but choose not to be their critic. Then we can move back into the present moment where we can be present with God, the place where his help and power are available to us!

Mindlessness, in contrast, makes us lose focus and rely on habit. We fail to notice our thoughts and emotions or what is going on around us. We do things without even thinking about them, making it easier to mindlessly start down the anxiety path. The distraction of anxiety will then keep us from noticing where God is and what he is doing in our present moment.

Since we have so many things to do in a day's time, we often attempt to handle a number of tasks at the same time. But multi-tasking is an enemy of mindfulness. Studies show that our brain cannot focus on multiple tasks, but instead chooses which task to place its focus on and then suppresses the others. Or our brain will move from task to task, hindering us from effectively focusing on any one of them. It is very easy for multi-tasking to become a hindrance to our relationship with God because we it becomes harder and harder to be present with just God since our mind is pulled in so many directions.

Questions that can be helpful to ask when you are feeling anxious are: "God where are you in this situation?" "What are you up to right now?" It is helpful to look at how God is using these situations in your life for good.

**Music: Its Power**

The vibrations of music can affect your physical body, your cells, and your mood. Some music relaxes you, some tends to excite you, some may inspire, while still others may even irritate you. In addition, singing is connected to your breath, which gives you two benefits at once (see comments on breath above).

Remember, just as junk food can increase stress and toxicity in your system, so can unhealthy music and sounds. Pick peaceful, soothing music if you want to relax more naturally. For more information on healthy and unhealthy sounds, read Gwen Ebner's book on Amazon, "Turning OFF Noise; Tuning IN to Healthy Sound."

**Music: Listen to It**

You can find music on YouTube, iTunes, or Amazon, as well as purchasing CDs. Here are some songs that we have found helpful for refocusing during times of anxiety:

*Be Still and Know, Steven Curtis Chapman*

*Be Still My Soul (in You I Rest)*, Kari Jobe
*Do What You Want To*, Vertical Church Band
*God is*, Hillsong
*Healer*, Kari Jobe
*Lord, I Need You*, Matt Maher
*Need You Now*, Plumb
*Pure*, Gateway Worship
*Sovereign Over Us*, Aaron Keyes
*The More I Seek You*, Gateway Worship
*Trust in You*, Lauren Daigle
*Turn your Eyes Upon Jesus*, Michael W. Smith
*You Alone*, Kim Hill
*You Are for Me*, Kari Jobe
*Wonderful Peace*, Candy Christmas

**Music: Sing and Play It**

You can sing a cappella (i.e. without any musical accompaniment), or with a recording, or you can make up your own song. If you can play an instrument, doing so can help shift your thought patterns and mood.

**Music: Move to It**

You can exercise to music (walk, run, aerobics, stretching, yoga, dancing, etc.). Or you might want to try creating a Dance to a worship song that inspires you; you can get two powerful benefits out of one activity (movement and listening to music).

**Physical Exercise**

- Physical Exercise can produce endorphins (chemicals in the brain) that can act as natural painkillers. They can improve your ability to sleep and boost your overall mood.
- Find a type of Exercise that you enjoy (or are willing to do); then exercise at least 3-4 days a week, 30-45 minutes
- Choices: Walking outside in nature, speed walking, yoga or stretching, biking, swimming, and exercises on machines at a gym or at home
- A different type of exercise is massage which releases muscle tension and helps you relax

**Practices that can be Helpful**

**Hand Position**

This practice can be helpful to do when you get anxious or find yourself focusing on your problems. (Your right hand represents a focus on Christ. Your left hand represents your anxiety or problem.)

1. Begin by putting your left hand "right in front" of your face (palm forward)
2. Then put your right hand behind that left hand (If your right hand represents Christ, how

much of him can you see when you are focused on your left hand or your problem? Not much, right?)
3. Now, exchange the position of your hands (move right hand "in front" of your face and left hand behind it). How much of your anxiety or problem (left hand) can you see now? Very little, right?

The next time you realize you have begun to focus on your anxiety, simply put your hands in front of your face and exchange the position of your hands so that Christ is right before your face. Then change your mind focus, too, from your anxiety to a focus on Christ. It will help your anxiety dissipate!

**Feel it and Let it Go**

Here is another practice that can be helpful. It is best to do this as soon as you recognize that you are full of emotion, such as anger, anxiety, frustration, fear, etc.

1. First, scan your body in your mind (Where in your body do you feel the emotion the most?)
2. Now, put your hand on the place where you feel the emotion
3. As you take in some calming breaths, inwardly acknowledge the emotion you are feeling (i.e. I am feeling really angry right now)

4. Stay in that position for a minute or two (with your hand on your body)
5. Then say, "I let this emotion go and give it to you, God"
6. Generally, once you've acknowledged it, felt it, and let it go, you feel differently
7. If you don't acknowledge, feel, and let it go, it will come back up to the surface over and over until you deal with it

**Sleep**

Sleep may be the most underrated exercise we partake of with a connection to beneficial hormones like serotonin (which calms you down) and melatonin (which helps reduces stress). Sleep is also very important in helping us handle stress. TheShawnStevensonModel.com/sleep-problems-tips website is able to offer you some helpful thoughts about sleep.

Here are a few ideas:

- Get more sunlight during the day, which can help the body sleep better at night
- Get a better night's sleep by avoiding too much blue light in the 90 minutes before bedtime, which produces more daytime hormones (i.e. TV, cell phones, computers, etc.)

- Take electronics out of your bedroom because they can give off radiation that will disrupt your sleep
- Darken your room as much as possible because light sources can disrupt your sleep patterns
- The ideal temperature for sleeping is around 68 degrees
- Go to bed at a similar time every night (our bodies have a way of knowing that it is time to sleep when it is dark and time to wake up when it is light)

**Thankfulness**

1. When you become aware of your anxious thoughts, immediately begin giving thanks to God for anything and everything you are grateful for
2. You can also speak or pray scriptures about gratitude allowing God's Word to form your thankfulness (Ps. 100:4, Ps. 95:2)
3. A second way to use the practice of thankfulness is to sit in God's presence adoring him, delighting in him, (Ps. 37:4) and expressing your love to him
4. A final way is to simply shut your eyes and enjoy the presence of the Lord in complete silence. (if you find your mind drifting back to

your concerns, gently return your attention to Jesus by saying his name)

**Your Environment**

Here are a few tips for creating a peaceful environment in your home:

- Hang pictures of peaceful scenes on your walls
- Create an electronics-free place in your home, a place where you can sit quietly away from the noise and confusion
- Paint your walls with peaceful colors
- Use house plants to create a peaceful environment; they will also help clean the air of toxic chemicals
- Use warm lighting, natural light, and lights made especially for seasonal disorders and moods
- Create a sense of calm by using an indoor table fountain or play a CD that has the relaxing sound of water

**Color Yourself Calm**

Coloring has been scientifically proven to change your brain and to help you feel calmer. Download free Scripture coloring pages to decrease anxiety here: www.livingcolorsonline.com/free

# REFERENCES

[1] Heidi Hanna, Stressaholic: 5 Steps to Transform your Relationship with Stress (Hoboken: NJ, 2014), loc. 139.

[2] Tony Jones, The Sacred Way (Grand Rapids, MI: Zondervan, 2005), 51.

[3] Hugh Feiss, Essential Monastic Wisdom: Writings on the Contemplative Lifestyle (San Francisco: Harper, 1999), 21.

[4] Michael Casey, Sacred Reading: The Ancient Art of Lectio (Liguori, Missouri: Liguori Publications, 1997), 83.

[5] Ibid.

[6] This came from a seminar with Thom Gardner called, "Restored Life Seminar."

[7] Contemplative Outreach, "About Lectio Divina," http://www.centeringprayer.com/Lectio_divina.html [accessed October 6, 2016].

[8] Jones, 54.

[9] Foster 1988, 27.

[10] Ibid.

[11] Mardel Christian Bookstore/ Mardel Education Homeschool Church Supplies, Inc., "Bible Translation Guide,"http://www.mardel.com/bibleTranslationGuide[accessed July 20, 2016].

[12] Maggie and Duffy Robbins, Enjoy the Silence (Grand Rapids, MI: Zondervan, 2005), 16.

# OTHER RESOURCES

**Books about anxiety**

- William Backus, Finding Freedom from Anxiety and Worry
- Annie Cole and Michael Ross, Seven Secrets of Worry-Free Living: Finding Freedom from Fear, Anxiety, and Stress
- Tony Evans, Let it Go: Breaking Free from Fear and Anxiety
- Timothy Lane, Living Without Worry: How to Replace Anxiety with Peace
- Phanuel Murerengwi, The Little Book on Worry: A Christian Perspective
- Jocelyn Wallace, Anxiety and Panic Attacks
- Edward T. Welch, Running Scared: Fear, Worry & the God of Rest
- Edward Welch, When I am Afraid: A Step-by-Step Guide Away from Fear and Anxiety by Edward T. Welch [a Workbook]

**Find a Counselor**
(Look online for these organization's websites to find a counselor)
- American Association of Christian Counselors
- Focus on the Family
- Psychology Today

# ABOUT THE AUTHOR

**Visit Gwen Ebner's Website, "Path to Wholeness" for more encouragement here:**
www.gwenebner.com

**Other Books by Gwen Ebner**

*Available on Amazon.com.*

- Formed Holy in his Image: Spirit, Soul and Body
- Intimate Moments with the Father: Connecting with God in Mind and Heart
- Turning OFF Noise; Tuning IN to Healthy Sound

**Download a Free Prayer Journal**

Download a free prayer journal with nine more scriptures for practicing Lectio Divina. You'll also get an audio so you can listen to a sample Lectio Divina session.

Get access now here: www.gwenebner.com/free